52 Weekend Decorating Projects

52 Weekend Decorating Projects

A Do-It-Yourself Guide to Adding Style to Your Home

Edited by Jean Nayar

Woman's Day® Specials

filipacchi
publishing

First published in the United States of America by
Filipacchi Publishing
1633 Broadway
New York, NY 10019

Design and art direction by Patricia Fabricant
Proofreading by Judith M. Gee

Woman's Day Specials and *Woman's Day Special Interest
Publications* are registered trademarks of Hachette Filipacchi
Media U.S, Inc.

ISBN: 2-85018-833-6

Printed in China

contents

introduction

DECORATING A HOME IS ABOUT finding personal style—defining an environment that sustains your spirits and reflects who you are and what you value. It is not so much an exercise in creating a certain look or style as it is a process of self-discovery. When faced with the blank slate of an empty room or one that's loaded down with layers of unrelated furnishings, choosing the ingredients for a tasteful space and figuring out how to put them together can be bewildering.

But breathing life into a stale or empty room doesn't have to involve an expensive overhaul. An honest assessment of your daily routines and some judicious editing of the things you have can yield fresh insight into how to build character into your rooms. When you preserve only what is important and conscientiously add what is missing, you create a room that is as practical as it is comfortable and pleasing to the senses.

Turning your attention toward refinishing an old table, repurposing an unmatched shutter, or creating a cluster of comfortable cushions rewards you not just with the pleasure of adding new, useful, and attractive elements to your room, but also gives you the satisfaction that creative self-expression brings. Such resourcefulness also helps you save money. If improving your rooms on a budget is your goal, the year's worth of weekend projects in this book is sure to provide the help and inspiration you'll need to achieve it.

custom furniture

WANT TO BREAK FREE OF A cookie-cutter look in your rooms? Then liven up the atmosphere with a one-of-a-kind piece of furniture. If you craft it yourself, a made-to-order table or dresser won't just make a personal statement—it will save you a bundle, too.

You don't necessarily need a workshop full of tools to create a customized piece. Many of the projects on the pages that follow require little more than a paintbrush or a pair of scissors and a staple gun to complete. You can make some of them using items you may already have on hand—or can easily find at a flea market or salvage shop. Others can be fashioned from scratch using low-cost staples like wallpaper remnants or lattice strips.

It's easy to add some cheer to a kitchen by simply reupholstering old barstools or to freshen a family room by resurfacing a tired side table. You can also redefine a dining room or give a bedroom a whole new look with more substantial pieces, like a crackle-finished sideboard or a brand-new headboard. Whether your style is cool and contemporary, down-to-earth country, traditional or dyed-in-the-wool romantic, there's a project here for you.

Painted Decoupage Dresser

MATERIALS
- dresser
- screwdriver
- 180-grit sandpaper
- tack cloth
- primer
- paintbrushes
- semigloss latex paint in two colors
- tape measure
- wallpaper
- scissors
- liquid adhesive or all-in-one sealer
- foam brush
- satin polyurethane

DIRECTIONS

1 Remove drawers from dresser. Using screwdriver, remove drawer hardware.

2 Sand dresser to smooth previous paint or finish, and wipe off dust with tack cloth.

3 Apply a coat of primer. Let dry.

4 Apply two coats of the lighter shade of paint to the dresser, letting dry between coats. Apply two coats of the darker shade of paint to the drawers, letting dry between coats.

5 Measure height and width of drawers. The width of the wallpaper diamond patterns should equal ¼ width of drawers, height should equal height of drawer. *NOTE: The top of our unit contains two drawers that are shorter than the bottom drawers. For consistency, we cropped the diamonds on the top level to align with the patterns on the lower drawers.*

6 Measure, mark, and cut four diamonds of wallpaper for each drawer. Cut one diamond for each row in half to position at ends of drawers.

7 Prior to applying cutouts, lay them on the drawer front, centering one diamond, flanking it by two others, and placing the cut halves of one diamond on the ends.

8 Use foam brush to apply adhesive to back of cutouts. Position cutouts in place on drawer fronts and hold several minutes, smoothing out bubbles. Let dry. Apply a coat of polyurethane to drawer fronts. Reattach hardware.

Country Sideboard

[SKILL LEVEL: BEGINNER]

MATERIALS

- glass-doored sideboard or hutch
- 180-grit sandpaper
- tack cloth
- disposable plastic plates
- acrylic paint in yellow, red, cream and burgundy
- 2-inch foam brushes
- crackle medium
- checked contact paper, wrapping paper or wallpaper remnant
- pencil
- craft knife
- metal ruler
- spray glue adhesive
- satin interior varnish

DIRECTIONS

1 Remove shelves and glass from doors of sideboard or hutch.

2 Sand inner and outer surfaces and both sides of shelves lightly, then remove dust with tack cloth.

3 Pour yellow and red paints (or the paint colors of your choice) onto separate plates. Using foam brush, paint shelves yellow. Let dry. Paint rest of cabinet, except for inside back, red.

4 Pour crackle medium onto plate. Following label instructions, coat shelves and cabinet, except for inside back, with crackle medium. Let dry.

5 Pour cream and burgundy paints (or the paint colors of your choice) onto separate plates. Paint shelves cream, and the sideboard, except for inside back, burgundy. Let dry.

6 Using a pencil, metal ruler and craft knife, measure, mark, and cut wallpaper or other paper to fit interior back of sideboard; apply spray glue to back of paper and press into place in back of cabinet, carefully smoothing to avoid wrinkles.

7 Varnish the entire cabinet, except for the papered surface, to finish.

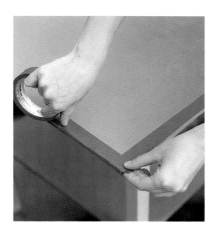

Bold Table

[SKILL LEVEL: BEGINNER]

DIRECTIONS

1 If table has a drawer, remove it. Using screwdriver, remove drawer hardware. Sand table; wipe off dust with tack cloth. Apply two coats of lightest paint to sides, legs, and drawer front. Apply two coats of darkest paint to top, shelf, and drawer pull. Let dry. Apply 1-inch-wide tape along outer edges of tabletop.

2 Apply tape across tabletop to form rectangles in assorted sizes. Paint insides of some rectangles with medium-tone paint; paint remaining rectangles with light paint. Remove tape while paint is wet. Let rectangles dry.

3 Apply tape near edges of each rectangle to create irregular borders between ¼ inch and 1½ inches wide. Paint borders to contrast with center of rectangle. Remove tape while paint is wet. Let dry. Apply two coats of sealer to all surfaces. Reattach drawer pull.

MATERIALS
• table
• screwdriver
• 180-grit sandpaper
• tack cloth
• acrylic paint in three shades of green
• paintbrushes
• 1-inch-wide painter's tape
• acrylic sealer

Faux Marquetry Pedestal Table

MATERIALS

- small table
- 180-grit sandpaper
- tack cloth
- primer
- semigloss paint in two complementary colors
- 2-inch paintbrushes
- metal ruler or yardstick
- circular cutter
- roll of cork liner
- roll of kraft paper
- cylindrical drinking glass or can about 3 to 4 inches in diameter
- pencil
- scissors
- tape
- sponge
- satin polyurethane

DIRECTIONS

1 If your table already has a painted or stained finish, sand it until smooth, then wipe off dust with tack cloth.

2 Apply one or two coats of primer, letting dry, sanding between coats and wiping off dust with tack cloth. Apply a coat of the darker color of paint, let dry. Sand lightly, wipe with tack cloth. Apply another coat of paint, let dry.

3 Measure the diameter of your table top. Using a circular cutter, cut the cork liner in a circular shape two inches smaller in diameter than the tabletop. Cut a circular piece of kraft paper to the same size. If your table also has a lower level, repeat this process for the surface of the lower level, too.

4 Peel off backing of the cut piece of cork liner and center it on top of table, pressing into place. Repeat for the lower level if your table has one.

5 To create a starburst stencil, place the cylindrical drinking glass or can in the center of the circle of kraft paper, using the ruler to be sure it's positioned precisely in the center. Trace around it with a pencil. Fold the circle in half with the traced circle facing out. Then fold it in half again, and then again, until it's shaped like a wedge. Use scissors to cut along the interior curved line. Using straight-edge, mark an angled line along both straight edges, starting at center of inner rounded edge and ending at about ¼ inch from outer rounded edge. Cut through all folds along both lines and open paper circle to reveal starburst form. Repeat for lower level if your table has one.

6 Place stencil over cork form and secure it to the tabletop, using a little tape.

7 Pour a small amount of the other shade of paint into dish, dip sponge into paint, and apply paint into stencil opening. Let dry. Remove stencil. Repeat for the lower level if your table has one.

8 Apply a coat of polyurethane over the entire table, including the stenciled cork. Let dry.

Folding Screen

DIRECTIONS

1 Sand surface of screen to smooth any previous finish or paint. Wipe off dust with tack cloth. Apply primer; let dry.

2 Apply a base coat of lightest paint color to screen and frame; let dry.

3 Paint interior of panels with the medium shade of paint; let dry.

4 To determine size of wallpaper insets, measure interior panels and subtract 4 to 5 inches from length and width to allow for borders all around. Using a straightedge and pencil, mark these dimensions on the wallpaper, using paperweights to hold paper down as you measure and mark. Cut out wallpaper insets.

5 Using a foam brush, apply adhesive to back of each wallpaper panel and center on each panel of screen, smoothing out any wrinkles.

6 As a final touch, apply painter's tape about ½ inch from inside of frame around inset all around. Apply the darkest shade of paint to this ½-inch outer border, let dry; remove tape.

MATERIALS
- unfinished or used folding screen
- 180-grit sandpaper
- tack cloth
- paintbrushes
- primer
- paint in three colors
- wallpaper
- metal yardstick
- pencil
- paperweights
- scissors
- foam brush
- liquid adhesive or all-in-one sealer
- painter's tape

Soda Fountain Stool

MATERIALS

- metal barstool with upholstered seat
- 220-grit sandpaper
- tack cloth
- paintbrush
- metal primer
- hot-pink acrylic paint
- tape measure
- cotton batting
- scissors
- heavy-duty stapler
- ¾ yard of printed oilcloth or cotton canvas fabric
- 1¼ yards of coordinating ½-inch-wide ribbon
- upholstery tacks

DIRECTIONS

1 Sand barstool; wipe off dust. Apply a coat of primer to base; let dry. Sand again; wipe off dust with tack cloth. Apply two or more coats of paint to base, letting dry after each coat.

2 Cut a circle of batting about 8 inches larger than seat all around. Center batting on seat; wrap and staple opposite sides under seat, pulling taut. Continue working from side to side to finish. Trim excess batting.

3 Cut a circle of fabric in the same size as batting. Center and staple fabric under seat in the same manner, pleating fabric around sides of seat as you go. Trim excess fabric.

4 Cut ribbon long enough to wrap around side of seat with 1-inch overlap. Wrap it around side of seat, securing it every few inches with upholstery tacks.

Stenciled Headboard

DIRECTIONS

1 Starting from baseboard, measure desired height of headboard and mark two vertical lines on wall, aligned with each side of your bed. Use carpenter's level to keep lines even. Measure and mark desired width of headboard across the top, using square to keep corners even.

2 Apply tape along outside of marked lines.

3 Apply two or three coats of background paint to taped-off area of wall, letting dry after each coat. Remove tape.

4 Spray back of stencil with adhesive; place on painted area of wall, allowing stencil to extend past an edge, if desired. Dip tip of stencil brush in contrasting paint, then lightly apply paint over openings in stencil, using a pouncing motion. Work from center of each cutout area toward edges to keep edges sharp. Remove stencil; let paint dry.

MATERIALS
- tape measure
- carpenter's level
- carpenter's square
- pencil
- painter's tape
- latex paint in two contrasting colors
- paintbrush
- stencil
- spray-on stencil adhesive
- stencil brush

Gingham-Backed Garden Gate Headboard

[SKILL LEVEL: BEGINNER]

MATERIALS

- wooden gate with decorative wood trim
- fine-grit sandpaper
- tack cloth
- latex paint
- paintbrush
- 2 yards of gingham fabric
- heavy-duty stapler
- scissors
- screwdriver
- two heavy-duty picture-hanging loops with screws and wire
- large nail
- hammer

DIRECTIONS

1 Sand all surfaces of gate; remove dust with tack cloth.

2 Apply two or three coats of paint in a color that complements your fabric to all surfaces of gate, letting dry after each coat.

3 Place gate wrong side up on a work surface. Place fabric face-down over gate so ends extend evenly all around. Staple fabric to gate, starting in center of each side and pulling fabric taut. Work from side to side to keep tension even as you staple. Cut away excess fabric.

4 Screw large picture hangers to sides of back of headboard, several inches below one long edge. Slip wire through loops, pulling taut. Wrap wire ends around wire to secure.

5 Attach nail to wall above center of bed; hang headboard on nail.

custom furniture

Portrait Gallery Headboard

DIRECTIONS

1 Sand door; remove dust with tack cloth. Apply a coat of primer to all surfaces; let dry.

2 Apply two or three coats of paint to all surfaces, letting dry after each coat.

3 Measure and mark desired placement of photographs. Using tape, attach photographs to door where marked.

4 Center Plexiglas over each photograph; screw in place at each corner.

5 Screw large picture hangers to back of headboard, several inches from upper edge near each side. Slip wire through loops, pulling taut. Wrap wire ends around center wire. Trim excess wire.

6 Attach nail to wall above center of bed; hang headboard on nail.

MATERIALS

- hollowcore door
- fine-grit sandpaper
- tack cloth
- wood primer
- latex paint
- paintbrush
- tape measure
- double-sided adhesive tape
- three 12x18-inch pieces of Plexiglas with a hole drilled in each corner *(see Note)*
- three photographs or prints
- 12 small silver screws
- screwdriver
- two heavy-duty picture-hanging loops with screws and wire
- large nail
- hammer

NOTE: A home-supply store can cut the Plexiglas to size and drill the holes for you.

Framed Wallpaper Headboard

[SKILL LEVEL: BEGINNER]

MATERIALS

- tape measure
- carpenter's level
- pencil
- carpenter's square
- 1x2-inch strips of wood trim
- handsaw
- fine-grit sandpaper
- tack cloth
- polyurethane
- paintbrush
- prepasted wallpaper
- scissors
- hand drill with bits
- decorative drawer pull
- hot-glue gun
- framed picture
- two small picture-hanging loops with screws
- 2 yards of 2-inch-wide ribbon
- double-sided foam tape

DIRECTIONS

1 Starting from baseboard, measure desired height of headboard and mark a line on wall, using carpenter's level to keep line even. Measure and mark desired width of headboard, using carpenter's square to keep corners even.

2 Cut a piece of trim to fit upper and side edges of marked area.

3 Sand all edges of trim; remove dust with tack cloth. Apply several coats of sealer to all surfaces of trim, letting dry after each coat.

4 Apply wallpaper to marked area of wall, following manufacturer's directions. If you need to use more than one piece of wallpaper, be sure to center seam and match pattern along seam.

5 Mark and drill small pilot hole at center of upper trim piece. Attach drawer pull at hole.

6 Glue trim to edges of wallpaper, butting ends together tightly at corners.

7 Screw small picture hangers to back of picture frame. Slip ribbon through loops, then tie ends in bow. Slip bow over drawer pull to hang picture.

8 Place small piece of foam tape on back of picture; remove tape backing and press to secure picture to headboard.

Canopy Headboard

DIRECTIONS

1 Spray the wreath lightly with white paint for a snow-frosted look; let dry.

2 Cut the ribbon in half. Attach a safety pin to one end of one piece of ribbon, then slide the ribbon through the rod pocket of the panel, pulling the pin through the pocket and gathering the panel as you go along until you pull the ribbon through the other side. Then repeat with the other panel.

MATERIALS

- 10-inch ready-made wreath of artificial willow leaves *(or another style of your own choosing)*
- white spray paint
- 2 yards of matching 1-inch-wide ribbon
- scissors
- safety pin
- two sheer organza curtain panels
- large nail
- hammer

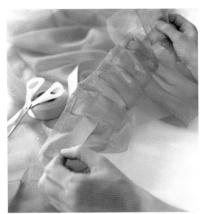

3 Tie the ribbon of one panel around the lower edge of the wreath, slipping the ribbon between the leaves. Attach the other panel in the same manner. Trim the excess ribbon. Mark the nail placement on the wall, centering it 4 to 6 feet above the bed. Pound the nail into the wall, slip the wreath over the nail, then arrange the panels as desired.

window dressing

NO WINDOW IS COMPLETE WITH-
out a dressing. And now that simpler, less-fussy treatments are taking center stage, it's easier than ever to create affordable, custom-designed curtains or shades yourself.

If you have basic sewing skills, the options are virtually endless. Do you like minimalist treatments? Then try a simple Roman shade made of fabric in a solid color or classic stripe. Looking for something with a little more panache? Just finish off the edge of a Roman shade with a lively scallop, or try a shaped valance. If casual comfort rules in your home, whip up a pair of sunny café curtains, add a ribbon border and clip-on rings, and hang them in a kitchen or bedroom window to add color and softness while controlling sunlight. Super-easy, soft-as-a-whisper sheers can bring a romantic fairy-tale quality to a room. Or, when left ungathered, they can make sleek panels for a pared-down contemporary look. Sheers are practical, too—they let in diffused light while providing privacy.

If you've never sewn a stitch, that's OK too. There are plenty of no-sew alternatives here. Consider making a simple accordion shade from a sheet of oversize colored paper. Or, craft a slatted shade from painted lattice strips. If you really want a fabric treatment, make reversible panels using fusible web—or simply hang a pair of tea towels, place mats, or tablecloths on a rod with clip-on rings for the easiest no-sew treatments possible.

Café Curtains

DIRECTIONS

1 Mount curtain rod in window at desired height.

2 Measure desired length of curtain (starting about 1½ inches below rod to allow for ring length). Measure width of window, divide this measurement in half and add 4 inches. Cut two pieces of fabric to these measurements.

3 Cut two pieces of each ribbon equal to width of each curtain plus 1 inch. Pin and stitch the wide ribbon about 5 inches from one edge of each panel, folding ends over to back at edges. Sew other ribbon to border about ½ inch from first ribbon.

4 Fold and press ½-inch double hems along sides, pin and sew side in place next to the folded edge. Then turn under and press ½-inch double hems along upper and lower edges and sew in place in same manner to finish hemming curtains.

5 Attach clips to upper edges of curtains, placing one at each upper corner and spacing remaining clips evenly about 6 inches apart. Hang curtains on rod.

MATERIALS
- curtain rod and mounting hardware
- 1½ yards of cotton decorator fabric
- yardstick
- scissors
- 1½ yards of ribbon in two colors as desired, ½ inch wide and 2 inches wide
- iron
- ironing board
- thread to match ribbon and curtain fabric
- sewing machine
- curtain clips

Gingham Roman Shade

MATERIALS

- tape measure
- metal ruler
- pencil
- decorator fabric
- lining
- scissors
- pins
- sewing machine with zipper foot
- thread
- ring tape
- piping cord
- needle
- staple gun
- thread
- screw eyes
- cord pull
- 1×2 mounting board cut to fit finished shade
- drill with ⅛-inch bit
- 2- or 3-inch wood screws
- screwdriver
- shade cleat

DIRECTIONS

1 Measure inside width and height of window frame. Measure, mark, and cut fabric 4 inches wider by 1 inch longer than the measurements. Cut lining to measurements that equal the inside length of the window, plus 1 inch by the inside width of the window. For valance, cut fabric equal to width of unfinished shade by ⅕ of finished shade length plus 3 inches. Cut lining to finished shade width by ⅕ of finished shade length plus 3 inches.

2 On shade lining, mark two vertical lines, evenly spaced apart at about 9 inches in from the side edges of the shade. *NOTE: For windows 36 inches wide or less, you will need to draw only one vertical line down the center of the lining.*

3 Pin ring tape, cut to fit, in place along side hems and marked lines, making sure rings line up horizontally. Sew tape to lining fabric only.

4 Center lining over decorator fabric, wrong sides together on a flat surface, pin and baste at top and bottom to secure. Repeat for valance.

5 Turn under and press a 1-inch double-fold hem along side edges of shade and blind hem stitch in place, stopping short 1 inch from bottom hem and leaving bottom hem open. Repeat for valance.

6 To make scalloped edge, divide bottom edge into sixths and draw six even scallops on lining side. Repeat for valance. Cut scalloped edges.

7 Cut two strips of piping cord, each long enough to cover scalloped edges. From decorator fabric, cut several 2-inch-wide strips of fabric on the bias. Square off short ends of strips and sew together with ½-inch seams to form one continuous casing, long enough to cover the piping cord. Wrap casing over piping cord, right side out, raw edges matching, and stitch as close to cord as possible, using a zipper foot.

8 Turn shade inside out, right sides facing. Sandwich piping between lining and face fabric along scalloped edge, raw edges matching; pin in place. Cut piping cord at both finished side hems, opening casing and leaving 1 inch of fabric to extend past each end. Repeat for valance.

9 Stitch through lining, seam allowance of piping, and face fab-

ric, as close to cord as possible. Turn shade right side out, and hand tack side hem in place, folding under excess fabric as needed for neat side edges. Press. Repeat for valance.

10 On a flat surface, place valance on top of shade, right sides up, raw edges together, and pin in place. Sew valance and shade together with ½-inch seam. Finish raw edge with a zigzag stitch, clipping excess. Press shade and valance.

11 Position shade and valance over mounting board, aligning seam with back edge of board, and staple in place. Install screw eyes into underside of board, aligning them with each row of rings.

12 Place shade face down on a flat surface. Decide whether draw cord will hang on right or left side of shade. Tie cord on bottom ring of row on opposite side of draw. Thread cord through all rings of row and screw eye, then across through all screw eyes, extending cord about three-fourths the way down the draw side of shade. Repeat for remaining rows, threading through remaining top screw eyes, until complete. Thread cords through pull and knot together.

13 Drill starter holes through mounting board 3 inches from each end and about every 7 to 8 inches apart. Using wood screws, attach mounting board to top of window frame. Screw cleat to side of frame where desired.

Bordered Tab-Topped Panels

[SKILL LEVEL: BEGINNER]

DIRECTIONS

1 Measure length from top of frame to sill and width of outside window frame. Measure, mark, and cut two panels of decorator fabric to these measurements plus 1 inch.

2 Add 7 inches to the length measurement and 13 inches to the width measurement, and cut two panels from contrasting fabric to these dimensions.

3 Turn under and press 3½ inches along all sides of each of the larger panels toward wrong side of fabric. Turn and press ½ inch along long edges of smaller panels toward wrong side. Center smaller panel over larger, right sides facing. Pin long raw edges together and stitch in place. Repeat for other panel. Turn both panels right side out. Fold under and press ½ inch along raw edges of top and bottom of larger panels; then flatten out edges to form 3-inch borders. Fold in corners to miter; pin. Topstitch inner folded edges and mitered corners.

4 To make tie, cut a strip of fabric 1x12 inches. Fold tie in half lengthwise, wrong side facing, and press. Open tie, and fold in raw edges ¼ inch and press. Refold along first crease. Topstitch all around. Repeat for all ties—you should make enough ties for each panel to be spaced 6 to 8 inches apart, beginning and ending at side edges.

5 Press each tie in half crosswise, then open tie and pin folded edge in place at one side of panel ¼ inch below top. Repeat on other side. Continue pinning ties along top edge, evenly spacing them 6 to 8 inches apart. Repeat for other panel. Topstitch along top edge of both panels to secure ties in place.

MATERIALS
- tape measure
- metal ruler
- pencil
- decorator fabrics— one print, one solid
- scissors
- iron
- pins
- sewing machine
- thread

Tailored Sheer Panels

MATERIALS

- tape measure
- metal ruler
- pencil
- sheer fabric
- lining fabric
- scissors
- iron
- pins
- sewing machine
- thread
- sticky-back hook-and-loop tape
- needle

DIRECTIONS

1 Measure width of outside window frame, add 4 inches and divide by 2. Measure from top of window frame to floor and add 3 inches. Measure, mark, and cut two panels to these dimensions.

2 For top band, measure, mark, and cut two strips from sheer fabric and one strip from lining fabric, measuring 4½-inch-wide by the width of window frame plus 1 inch.

3 Turn under and press a ½-inch double fold hem along both side edges of both panels. Stitch in place with blind hem stitch. Turn under and press a 2-inch double-fold hem along bottom. Stitch in place with blind hem stitch.

4 Place lining on back side of one sheer top band, pin, and baste. Place panels side by side, right sides up, on work surface. Center long edge of basted top band, face down, over top edges of panels, matching raw edges. Pin in place; stitch top band to panels.

5 Cut a strip of hook-and-loop tape equal in length to window frame width. Peel off backing and attach loop portion of strip along center of right side of remaining top piece. Attach hook portion of tape along center of window frame top.

6 Position remaining top piece over basted top piece, right sides facing raw edges matching; pin in place. Sew around both short edges and long edge that's not attached to panels with a ½-inch seam allowance. Clip corners. Turn top piece right side out and press, fold under and press raw edge; hand-stitch stitch opening closed. Connect hook-and-loop strips to attach to window.

Simple Slatted Shade

[SKILL LEVEL: BEGINNER]

MATERIALS

- tape measure
- metal ruler
- pencil
- 2-inch-wide wood slats, cut to fit within window frame *(we used 3/32-inch-thick pieces of balsa wood, available at craft and art-supply stores)*
- 1/2-inch diameter wooden dowel, cut to fit within window frame
- saw or craft knife
- primer
- latex paint
- paintbrushes
- 6-ply embroidery floss or thin string or cord
- wood or other large-holed beads (3/8 to 1/2 inch in diameter)
- two 1/2-inch screw hooks

DIRECTIONS

1 Measure the inside width and height of your window frame. Determine how many slats you'll need by dividing the height of the window frame by 2½ minus 2 inches. Measure, mark, and cut wood slats (if using balsa wood slats, cut with craft knife) and dowel to width measurement minus ¼ inch.

2 Brush slats and dowel with primer on one side, let dry. Turn over and prime other sides, let dry. Repeat this process with latex paint—applying two coats if necessary and letting dry between coats.

3 Cut two pieces of embroidery floss, string, or cord equal in length to twice the inside length of window frame plus 8 inches. Fold one piece of string in half over the dowel about 2 inches from one end, and thread the ends through two beads. Open the ends of string, insert a slat between the open strings, close the strings, and thread through another bead. Repeat this process until all slats and beads are attached. After threading on last bead, knot the string two or three times to secure, and cut off excess string or floss. Repeat this process on other side of dowel.

4 If desired, paint screw hooks to match shade, let dry. Insert screw hooks to top of window frame about 2 inches in from either side; finish with hooks facing forward. Place dowel onto hooks to hang shade. To lift shade, pull bottom beads up and hang on hooks.

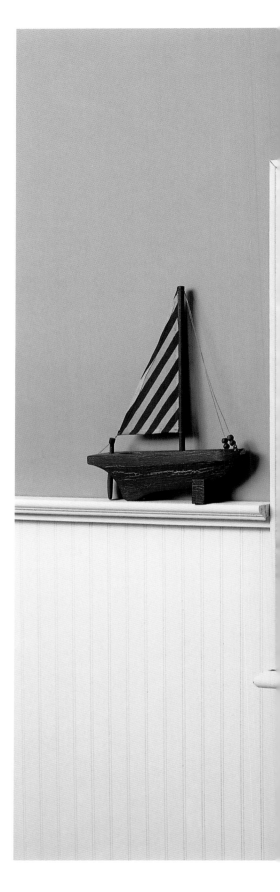

window dressing

Folded Shade

MATERIALS

- tape measure
- large sheet of pastel paper *(must be large enough to fit, or be cut to fit, your window width and length)*
- long metal ruler
- pencil
- craft knife or saw
- cutting mat
- 2-inch-wide mounting board or wood slat *(we used a 3⁄32-inch-thick piece of balsa wood, available at craft and art-supply stores)*
- glue or glue stick
- small hole punch
- eyelets
- eyelet tool
- hammer
- string
- screw eyes
- drill with 1⁄8-inch bit and screwdriver bit
- staple gun or wood screws
- cord pull
- shade cleat

DIRECTIONS

1 Measure width and height of inside window frame. Measure, mark, and cut paper to dimensions 1⁄4 inch shorter than width and 3 inches longer than height of inside window frame, using craft knife and straightedge. Cut two 1-inch-wide strips of paper equal to length of cut paper shade. Measure, mark, and cut wood slat or mounting board to length 1⁄4 inch shorter than inside frame width.

2 Spread a thin layer of glue to backs of 1-inch-wide paper strips and apply to side edges of back side of shade. On back side of shade, measure and mark lines across width of shade 1 inch apart from top to bottom. Using straightedge and back of craft knife, lightly score along each line, making sure not to cut through paper. Fold shade along scored lines in accordion pleats, sharply pressing creases.

3 Except in top pleat, punch small holes through center of 1-inch square of each pleat along both side edges. Insert eyelet through hole, place on cutting mat, and secure in place using eyelet tool and hammer—or follow manufacturer's instructions. Repeat until each hole contains a finished eyelet.

4 Making sure your string easily fits through the eyelets, cut one piece of string three times longer than and another piece two times longer than window frame height. Thread one piece of string through the eyelets along one side of shade, and the other piece through the eyelets on other side. Knot the string at the bottom of each side, leaving a 4-inch-long tail.

5 Glue back side of top pleat to wood slat. Insert screw eyes through center of slat, 1⁄2 inch in from either end, drilling starter holes if necessary. Drill starter holes in top of window frame to accommodate screw eyes, if necessary. Install shade in window, stapling or screwing mounting slat or board to frame.

6 Thread long piece of string through screw eye above, then across shade through opposite screw eye. Thread shorter string through screw eye above and let hang next to long piece. Adjust shade so it hangs evenly. Thread ends of string through a cord pull, knotting ends, and cut off excess. Install shade cleat on side of frame where desired.

7 Make tassel by wrapping string several times around three fingers to form loop. Tie loop together at one side with string; cut loop at bottom to form tassel ends. Wrap string around tassel top a few times and knot to secure. Then tie tassel onto tails at bottom sides of shade.

Clip-On Valance

MATERIALS

- tape measure
- metal ruler
- paper
- pencil
- kraft paper
- scissors
- pins
- decorator fabric
- lining
- piping cord
- thread
- sewing machine with zipper foot
- needle
- iron
- ironing board
- curtain clips
- curtain rod and brackets
- screwdriver

DIRECTIONS

1 Measure width of outside window frame and determine depth of valance from top to lowest point along bottom hem. Add 1 inch to both measurements and draw a rectangle to these dimensions on kraft paper. Cut out. Fold paper in half crosswise (short ends together). To make pattern, draw freehand a gentle curve along bottom edge to shape as desired, and cut along the marked line. Open pattern.

2 Pin pattern to fabric, centering over fabric repeat, and cut one valance piece. Repeat to create one lining piece.

3 Add together measurements of all four sides of valance plus 20 inches for curve, and cut a piece of piping cord to this length.

4 From decorator fabric, cut several 2-inch-wide strips of fabric on the bias. Square off the ends of strips and sew short ends together with ½-inch seams to form one continuous casing, long enough to cover the piping cord. Wrap casing over piping cord, right side out, raw edges matching, and stitch as close to cord as possible, using a zipper foot. Trim the raw edges to ½ inch.

5 Pin piping to valance face fabric, right side up, raw edges matching. Cut piping cord where ends meet so that they abut neatly, opening casing and cut fabric, leaving ½ inch of fabric to extend past each end of cord. Fold in one end of casing to finish and pin in place. Sew piping to valance using zipper foot. Remove pins.

6 Place lining fabric over face fabric, right sides facing and raw edges matching with piping sandwiched between, and pin in place. Stitch along all sides close to piping, leaving a 9-inch opening along top edge for turning. Remove pins.

7 Trim seams, turn right side out and press; hand-stitch opening closed.

8 Attach curtain clips to top of valance, spaced 6 to 8 inches apart. Mount brackets at desired position, thread clip along rod and set on brackets.

window dressing

Reversible Curtains

DIRECTIONS

1 Mount curtain rod where desired above window frame.

2 Measure width outside window frame and height from just below curtain rod to window sill. Divide width by 2 and add 1¼ inches, and add 1¼ inches to height measurement. Measure, mark, and cut two panels from each fabric to these dimensions.

3 Turn in and press side, bottom, and top edges of all panels ⅝ inch. Trim all corners on diagonal ¼ inch from folds. Turn in and press cut corners ¼ inch.

4 Measure the diameter of your curtain rod and multiply by 3½, and add 1½ inches. Cut strips of grosgrain or other ribbon to this length for curtain loops. You should cut enough strips for each finished panel to be spaced about 6 to 8 inches apart, beginning and ending at side edges, plus two more for corner pullbacks.

5 Fold loops in half. Cut twice as many ½-inch-wide pieces of fusible web as you have pieces of ribbon. Following manufacturer's instructions, iron on web to inside of one free end of each loop. Then press inside of remaining free end to the web to close each loop. Then iron a piece of web on outside of each closed loop near cut ends.

6 Cut two strips of web equal to width and length of finished panel for each panel. Following manufacturer's instructions, iron on strips of web to folded edges of front piece of each panel. Peel paper backing off web strips on each panel and off loops. Starting at side edges, evenly space loops along top edge with web side of loop facing up and raw edges aligned. Position reverse side of panel on top, aligning folded edges, and press top edge until all pieces are secured in place, following manufacturer's instructions. (You may have to press longer if your fabric is fairly heavy.) Position a loop at the outer lower corner of your panel, web side up, and continue pressing all around until your panel is completely secured. Repeat for other panel.

7 Thread your panels onto rod and mount. Draw back inner corners toward wall to determine placement of drawer pulls on your wall. Mark the point with a pencil, and screw in pulls. Loop pullbacks over drawer pulls.

MATERIALS
- curtain rod and brackets
- screwdriver or drill driver
- tape measure
- two kinds of complementary decorator fabric
- long metal ruler
- pencil
- scissors
- iron
- ironing board
- ½-inch-wide grosgrain or other cloth ribbon
- ⅝-inch-wide fusible iron-on web
- drawer pulls

Easy Sheer Panels

MATERIALS
- tape measure
- four to six sheer decorative place mats
- pins
- matching thread
- sewing machine
- hand-sewing needle (optional)
- curtain clips
- tension rod

DIRECTIONS

1 Measure the width and height of your window to determine the number of place mats you'll need to join to cover one half to two thirds of your window with a flat panel. When making your calculation, remember that the place mat borders will overlap in the center.

2 Pin two place mats together, overlapping two short edges, right sides facing up. Topstitch along both edges of the overlapping borders to join the panels. Repeat with two more panels, and two more, if necessary. If you want to stack two pairs of three place mats with the long edges running vertically, topstitch another place mat along the other short edge of one pair of joined panels, then repeat for the other pair.

3 Overlap the long edges of the joined panels, pinning in place. Topstitch along one edge of the overlapped borders, rolling over excess fabric to flow smoothly through the machine as you sew. If the layers are too thick for your sewing machine needle to pass through where all four borders overlap, lift the sewing machine foot, slide this section forward, and start sewing again where only two sections overlap. Hand-sew the central section closed with a slipstitch.

4 Apply curtain clips, evenly spaced, along either the long or short edge of panel as desired, then slide rings over rod. Install rod into place in window frame.

easy
sewing

N OTHING WARMS UP A ROOM like a sumptuous throw, a cozy coverlet or a mélange of comfy cushions. Soft furnishings like these don't just take the edge off hard surfaces, they actually cultivate the mood of a room with their colors, textures, and patterns.

When choosing fabrics for soft furnishings, consider the ambience you want to convey, then opt for a textile that mirrors that impression. If you desire a relaxed, casual tone in a family room, for example, make an ottoman slipcover from durable, easy-to-wash denim. For a soft, romantic air in a guest room, on the other hand, create a throw pillow or two from pretty organza.

The best thing about soft furnishings is the character and comfort they bring to your decor at so little cost. A chair seat cushion requires just half a yard of fabric, a bit of batting, and some thread. A patchwork quilt can be pieced together with remnants of worn pillowcases and sheets, outgrown clothes, or old window treatments. You can even fashion some throw pillows from a pair of place mats. For extra flourish, embellish fabrics with hand- or machine-embroidery. And don't forget the impact of trims: Add a little elegance with a satin ribbon border or a touch of wit with a zesty ball fringe.

Fringed Ottoman Cover

[SKILL LEVEL: BEGINNER]

MATERIALS

- ottoman
- tape measure
- yardstick
- chalk marking pencil
- scissors
- string
- tape or tack
- pins
- sewing machine with walking foot
- thread
- ball fringe

DIRECTIONS

1 Measure diameter of ottoman, or, if it's square or rectangular, measure its width and length. Measure and mark the fabric so that its diameter is 1¼ inch larger in diameter than the top of the ottoman, or if it's square or rectangular, 1¼ inch longer than both width and length measurements. To make a circular shape, cut a piece of string and tie one end to the chalk pencil. Measure half the length of the diameter along the string, and tape or tack string at that point to center of fabric. Holding the pencil straight up and down, pull the string taut as far as it will go without lifting the tape or tack, and mark a circle shape onto the fabric.

2 Cut out the top shape.

3 Measure circumference of ottoman and the height of its side (not including legs). Add 1¼ inch to both measurements and measure, mark, and cut a piece of fabric to these dimensions. *NOTE: The circumference of our ottoman was 68, and the side was 9¾ inches, so we cut a piece of fabric measuring 69¼x11 inches.* With right sides facing, pin ottoman skirt around top.

4 Where side ends meet, stitch closed using a ½-inch seam; trim off excess. Using a walking foot, stitch around top, attaching it to the skirt with ½-inch seam. Press seams open.

5 Topstitch along on both sides of seam around top to finish.

6 Turn and press bottom hem up ½ inch, then turn up ½ inch again and press to make a ½-inch double hem. Stitch in place.

7 Pin ball fringe around hem and stitch in place along bottom and top edges of trim.

Fringed and Trimmed Pillows

MATERIALS

- pillow forms *(we used 18- and 20-inch squares)*
- decorative denim, crewelwork, and corduroy fabrics *(or contrasting fabrics of your choice)*
- yardstick
- chalk marking pencil
- scissors
- pins
- sewing machine with zipper foot and walking foot
- iron
- ironing board
- thread
- hand-sewing needle
- fringe
- 2½ yards of corded piping

DIRECTIONS

1 To make 18-inch pillow with fringe: Measure, mark, and cut two 19-inch-square pieces of fabric.

2 Pin bound edge of fringe facing outside edges of right side of one piece of fabric. Using walking foot, stitch fringe to fabric ½ inch in from outside edge around all four sides (allow extra fringe at the corners).

3 Place pillow back, on top of front, right sides facing, sandwiching fringe between the layers. Pin in place and sew around all four sides, leaving a 7-inch opening along one side for turning.

4 Turn pillow cover right sides out, press. Insert 18-inch pillow form; slip stitch opening closed.

5 To make 20-inch pillow with cording: Measure, mark, and cut a 21-inch-square piece from crewelwork fabric and another from the corduroy.

6 Measure, mark, and cut 2½ yards of ¾-inch corded piping.

7 With raw edges aligned, pin piping to front fabric. Using zipper foot, stitch cording to fabric pillow using a ½-inch seam allowance (allow extra cording at the corners).

8 Place pillow back, right sides facing, over top, pin in place. Stitch around all four sides, leaving a 7-inch opening on one side for turning.

9 Turn pillow cover right sides out, press. Insert 20-inch pillow form and slip stitch opening closed.

10 To make 20-inch pillow with contrasting band flange: Measure, mark, and cut two 21-inch-square pieces of decorative denim fabric for pillow back and front.

11 Cut four 2½x22-inch strips of plain contrasting denim. Fold and press strips in half lengthwise.

12 Pin strips to form a square frame, inserting folded ends of side edges between top and bottom folded edges. Turn in corners of both sides of top and bottom at 45-degree angles, and topstitch to form mitered corners. Trim excess fabric at sewn corners.

13 Place flange over top, raw edges matching. Place pillow back over front, right sides facing and sandwiching flange between layers; pin in place. Sew all layers together around all four sides with ½-inch seam, leaving 7-inch opening for turning.

14 Turn pillow cover right side out, press. Insert 20-inch pillow form; slip stitch opening closed.

Reversible Denim Throw

DIRECTIONS

NOTE: All seams will be stitched with ¼-inch allowances unless otherwise stated. Also, the size of your throw will depend on how much bulk your machine can accommodate when you roll the fabric as you sew. To reduce bulk, forgo batting and the stippling of the plain denim.

1 From the assorted fabrics, measure, mark, and cut two 12½-inch squares from each fabric. Arrange squares to form two rows of five different squares. Then repeat these layouts for next two rows so you have four rows of five squares each.

2 Pin first row of five squares together and, using the ¼-inch foot, stitch pieces to form row. Press seams to the right. Pin and stitch second row of squares together. Press seams to the left. Repeat these steps for the next two rows.

3 Pin rows together, making sure seams from each row face in opposite directions (to reduce bulk). Using the pin feed foot, stitch rows together.

4 Using the zipper foot, baste ½-inch corded piping around edges of quilt top (6 yards total) at ¼ inch from outside edge.

5 Cut a 53x65-inch piece of backing fabric for the throw. Cut a 55x67-inch piece of thin quilt batting. Quilt batting to quilt back as desired (we used a free-motion stippling technique, using a free-motion foot). Trim excess batting around edges to ¼ inch within the edges of the backing fabric.

6 Lay backing right side up on table, layer quilt top over backing, right sides facing. Pin sections together, smoothing layers as you go so there are no wrinkles. Stitch around all four sides, using the zipper foot, leaving a 10-inch opening for turning quilt.

7 Turn quilt right sides out, press. Slip stitch opening closed.

8 Pin layers together and, using a darning needle, bar tack or tie with yarn at each intersection.

MATERIALS

- ten assorted denims and other complementary fabrics (½ yard each)
- 2 yards of plain denim
- yardstick
- chalk marking pencil
- scissors
- pins
- thread
- sewing machine with ¼-inch foot, pin feed foot, zipper foot, and free-motion foot
- thin batting *(optional)*
- 6 yards of ½-inch decorative corded piping
- iron
- ironing board
- hand-sewing needle
- darning needle
- yarn

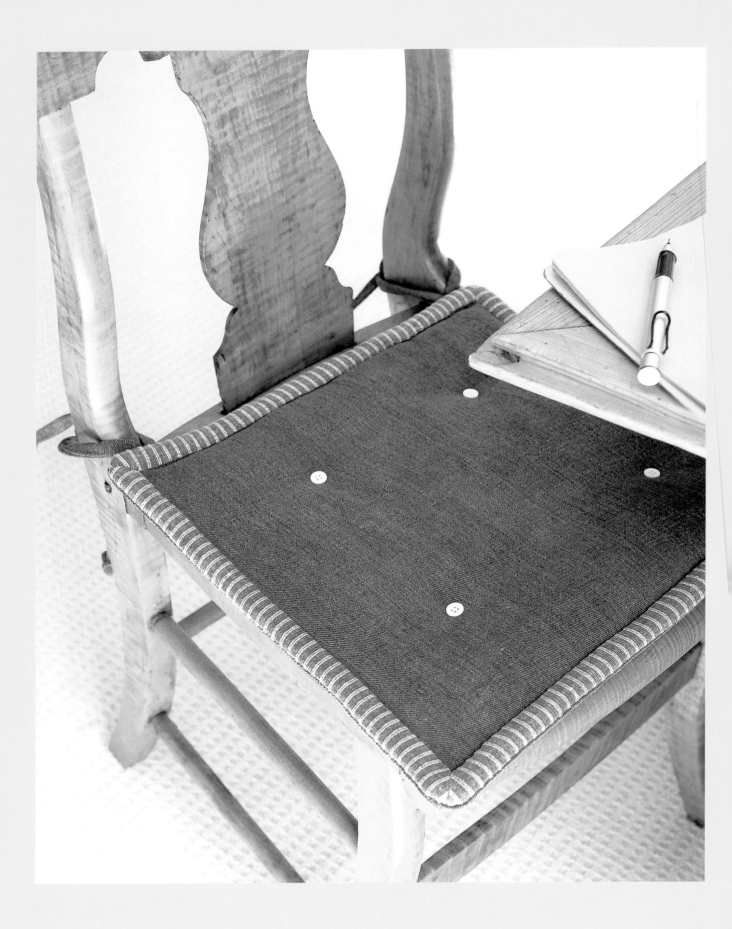

Chair Cushion

[SKILL LEVEL: BEGINNER]

DIRECTIONS

1 Measure front, sides and back of chair seat in front of chair back and add 1 inch to each measurement.

2 Measure, mark and cut two pieces to these dimensions from the plain fabric.

3 For the border, cut four 2½-inch strips equal in length to the front, sides, and back measurements plus 1 inch.

4 Press under one long edge of each strip ¼ inch, and place strips along edges of top with raw edges facing and right sides up. Pin borders to top along folded edge. Open up border and stitch to top all around along fold lines. Stitch corners together at 45-degree angles to miter. Clip excess fabric at corners.

5 Measure, mark and cut batting to same size as top and bottom covers. Lay batting onto wrong side of top and pin in place. From the front of the cushion, stitch in the ditch between the border and cushion top all around.

6 Cut four strips of 15x1½ inch of fabric to match pillow top and back. Fold and press in ¼ inch on each long edge. Fold in half again lengthwise and press, stitch edges closed to form four ties. Tie knots at one end of each tie to conceal raw ends.

7 Tack two ties in place on right side of cushion front, raw edges matching, at the back edge near both corners.

8 Lay cushion back on top of cushion front, right sides together. Pin and stitch around all four sides, leaving a 6-inch opening for turning. Turn cushion right sides out, press; slip stitch edges closed. Stitch in the ditch again to secure all layers.

9 Mark four points on the cushion top about 4 inches in from each side and from the back and the front. Hand-sew buttons at each point to create tufting.

MATERIALS
- chair
- tape measure
- plain and decorative denim fabrics
- yardstick
- chalk marking pencil
- scissors
- thick batting
- sewing machine
- thread
- buttons
- hand-sewing needle

Flanged Pillows

MATERIALS

- two place mats
- yardstick
- scissors
- 2 yards of grosgrain ribbon *(optional)*
- pins
- tailor's chalk
- matching thread
- sewing machine
- polyester fiber

DIRECTIONS

1 Measure the length and width of your place mat; add these two dimensions together, and multiply the sum by 2. Cut a piece of ribbon to this length.

2 Position one place mat on top of the other, back sides facing. Pin the top, bottom and sides together with one or two pins along each edge.

3 Using the yardstick and tailor's chalk, measure and mark a rectangle on the front of one place mat 1½ to 2 inches from the perimeter all around. Pin the ribbon over the marked rectangle, beginning at the corner of one long edge, folding the ribbon over itself at the corner to run perpendicular along a short edge, and continuing in this manner until the ribbon meets where it started. Fold the ribbon under at the final corner to conceal the raw edge and let it extend beneath the ribbon stretched along the first long edge about 1 inch. Cut any excess ribbon. *NOTE: If your place mat already has a border, forgo the ribbon and topstitch along the border's inner edges, leaving a 6-inch opening along one short edge.*

4 Starting about 2 inches from the end of one short edge, topstitch along one side of the ribbon toward the nearest corner, turn at the corner, and continue stitching all around until you reach 2 inches past the other corner along the short edge you started on, leaving a 6-inch opening on that side. Repeat this process, topstitching along the other edge of the ribbon.

5 Stuff polyester fiber into the cover through the opening. Topstitch along the ribbon's edges at the opening to close pillow cover.

Quilted Coverlet

MATERIALS

- 12 to 16 quilted place mats (*12 mats will yield a twin-size coverlet; 16 a full or queen; if you want a quilt, use 15 for a twin, 20 for a full or queen.*)
- 11 yards of 1-inch-wide ribbon
- scissors
- pins
- Scotch tape
- thread to match ribbon
- sewing machine or hand-sewing needle
- 1½ yards of 54-inch-wide poplin or old sheeting cut to 78x54 inches
- large-eyed embroidery needle
- 6-ply embroidery floss to match ribbon (*optional*)

DIRECTIONS

1 Place four place mats in a row, aligning their short ends, right sides facing up. Place another row of place mats, short ends aligned, adjacent to the first. Cut a 78-inch strip of ribbon (the ribbon will run the length of four place mats, which are generally 19 inches long each; other ribbons will be cut to run the width of four place mats, which are generally 13 inches wide—measure yours to be sure they're standard size, and if not, adjust the dimensions of the cut ribbons accordingly, adding 2 inches for folding over at ends).

2 Place the ribbon over the bound edges of the long sides of the two adjacent rows of place mats. Pin it in place to secure both rows together, folding the 1-inch excess at each end of the ribbon around to the back. Repeat Steps 1 and 2 with two more rows of four place mats each.

3 Apply strips of tape over the short edges of the place mats to temporarily secure them, or pin them together. Roll over one long edge of one set of pinned place mats, and topstitch the ribbon next to each long edge to secure the lengths of the place mats together. Repeat for the other set of pinned place mats.

4 Place each of the two sets of joined place mats next to each other, long sides aligning and right sides facing up. Cut another 78-inch piece of ribbon, and place the ribbon over the bound edges of the long sides of the two adjacent sets of place mats and pin in place. Again, roll up one side of the joined mats so that they flow under the sewing machine easily, then topstitch the ribbon along both long edges of the ribbon to join all of the mats along their lengths. Remove pins.

5 Cut three pieces of ribbon 54 inches long. Remove the tape or pins, securing the short sides of the mats. Then position the three strips of ribbon over the bound short ends of the adjacent mats, pinning in place and folding over the ends of the ribbon to the back. Topstitch these ribbons along both sides to secure all the place mats together. (Alternatively, all of the ribbons may be secured to the mats by hand, using a running stitch.) Remove pins.

6 Press under a 1-inch hem on all four sides of the poplin or sheeting. Turn the coverlet face side down on a surface, place the poplin or sheeting over the coverlet, wrong sides facing. Pin the poplin or

sheeting to the coverlet around all edges. Then turn over, and stitch in the ditch along the bound edges of the mats to secure backing to coverlet.

7 Secure the backing to the coverlet by hand-tufting with a large-eyed embroidery needle and embroidery floss, or with several layers of thread at ribbon intersections.

bright lights

EVERYONE APPRECIATES THE PRACtical value of light fixtures, but most of us overlook their decorative potential. Usually we select floor and table lamps with bases that complement our decor. You might choose a sleek, brushed-aluminum table lamp for your modern home office, a whitewashed turned wood floor lamp for your country house living room, or a whimsical wrought-iron lamp for a child's room.

Whatever size or shape your lamp bases may be, chances are their shades are simple cones of paper or plain fabric. If that's the case, then why not elevate their status with a little creative flair? Give a plain shade romantic flourish with an easy-to-make ruffled cotton topper. Or, switch out a cone-shaped shade on a modern base for a drum, square, or angled shade, then doll it up with strips of ribbon and a few crisp bows or fabric that matches your decor. Alternatively, you might want to create your own inventive shade for a pendant fixture from an acrylic bowl—or even a metal colander.

It's so easy—and inexpensive—to dress up a lampshade to bring a little punch to your decor.

Woven Shade

MATERIALS

- sixteen 1x7-inch strips of denim fabric
- Fray Check or other seam sealant
- hot-glue gun
- tapered shade with straight top and bottom edges
- eight 1x24-inch strips of denim fabric
- four pieces of red ribbon

DIRECTIONS

1 Take the sixteen 1x7-inch strips of denim fabric. Apply seam seal-ant along raw edges. Using hot-glue gun, adhere the tip of one strip to one side of the top rim of the shade. Repeat, until every side contains four dangling strips, with no spaces between.

2 Take the eight 1x24-inch strips of denim fabric. Apply seam sealant along raw edges. Starting at one top corner, weave the strip over and under each dangling vertical strip around the entire shade. Cut excess and glue in place. Repeat with each long strip, starting at same edge, interchanging over and under pattern, until shade is covered. Glue vertical strips down at bottom, trimming excess.

3 Cut four pieces of red ribbon—one to fit around the diameter of the top rim of your shade, two around the middle, and one around the bottom. Place glue around the top rim of the shade, and press a piece of ribbon firmly in place on top of it. Let dry. Repeat the gluing process on the rest of the shade, evenly spacing the following ribbons apart. Pick one side of the shade to highlight, add a drop of glue to the center of each ribbon, then press one small, pre-tied silk bow on each ribbon. Place your new shade on a small base.

Ruffled Shade Topper

DIRECTIONS

1 Measure length of shade frame; add 6 inches. Cut fabric equal in width to this measurement by 50 inches long.

2 Fold fabric in half crosswise, right sides facing and raw edges even. Pin and stitch short edges with ½-inch seam. Trim one seam allowance to ¼ inch. Turn in ¼ inch along wrong edge of other allowance; pin and stitch over trimmed allowance, enclosing raw edge.

3 Insert upper edge of fabric between folds of bias binding; pin and stitch close to edge of binding, turning under ½ inch on end before stitching it in place. Pin and stitch binding to lower edge of fabric in same manner.

4 Measure around upper edge of shade frame; cut elastic to this measurement. Overlap elastic ends ½ inch and stitch to form circle. Pin circle to wrong side of fabric, 2 inches from upper edge. Stretch elastic to fit; pleat fabric if needed. Stitch through center of elastic to secure it to fabric to form fabric shade.

5 Saturate shade with starch or stiffener. Place shade frame on lamp, then place shade on frame. Arrange fabric to form ruffle at upper edge and soft folds at lower edge. Use bottles to prop up lower edge so shade holds its shape. Let dry overnight. Remove bottles.

MATERIALS
- lampshade frame (or old shade with frame, with shade removed)
- tape measure
- 1½ yards of white cotton fabric
- white thread
- pins
- sewing machine
- iron
- ironing board
- 3 yards of double-fold bias binding in pink print
- matching thread
- ½ yard of ½-inch-wide elastic
- spray starch or fabric stiffener
- several bottles or drinking glasses

Ribbon-Trimmed Lampshade

MATERIALS

- paper lampshade
- tape measure
- about 4½ yards of ½-inch-wide picot-edge ribbon
- about 4 yards of ⅜-inch-wide satin ribbon
- scissors
- Fray Check or other seam sealant
- paper clips
- fabric glue

DIRECTIONS

1 Measure height of lampshade; cut about ten pieces of each color of ribbon to this measurement.

2 Alternating colors, clip one end of each ribbon strip to upper edge of shade, spacing as desired. Cut and clip more ribbons as needed.

3 Remove ribbons one by one, apply glue to wrong side, then press onto shade, smoothing it down so ends are evenly spaced.

4 Measure around upper edge of shade and add 1 inch; cut wider ribbon to this measurement. Glue this ribbon around upper edge of shade, covering upper ends of glued ribbons. Cut ends so they abut neatly, and apply seam sealant to them.

5 Measure around lower edge of shade and add 1 inch. Glue this ribbon in place and finish the same way as upper edge.

Pretty Pendant

DIRECTIONS

1 Drill hole in center bottom of colander to allow for insertion of lamp parts.

2 Lightly sand outside of colander; wipe off dust with tack cloth.

3 Place colander in a large box or protected area lined with newspaper. Spray primer on outside of colander. Let dry.

4 Spray paint on outside of colander. Let dry.

5 Install lamp kit and hang as directed by manufacturer's instructions.

MATERIALS

- metal colander
- drill with 5/16-inch bit
- hanging-lamp kit
- fine-grit sandpaper
- tack cloth
- white spray primer
- glossy spray paint
- screwdriver
- pendant lamp kit

all about accessories

AROOM MAY HAVE GREAT BONES and even great furniture, but without the accessories, it's just not finished. It's the little things—accents like planters or candle-holders—or sometimes even the not-so-little things—like bed linens or floorcloths—that give a space its character. Like shoes or handbags, accessories are easy to change—with the season or with your mood.

Think of them as an opportunity to express yourself. A floorcloth is just a floorcloth—until you paint one yourself in a palette of your favorite hues. Similarly, a simple sap bucket can become a beacon of your inventiveness if you drill it with holes in the shape of a starburst and convert it into a hurricane lamp.

Whether you're ambitious and make some accessories from scratch or you simply want to put your creative stamp on an accent piece you already have, inspiration and options abound. For example, let the colors of a printed pillowcase inspire your choice of a ribbon border. Take cues from nature and adorn a painted planter with seashells and starfish. Or, turn leaves into stencils by painting them on one side, then pressing their silhou-ettes onto a collection of cork coasters you craft yourself.

Canvas Floorcloth

MATERIALS

- floorcloth canvas
  (we cut ours to 4x6 feet)
- yardstick
- pencil
- scissors
- iron
- ironing board
- tacky glue
- 2-inch-wide painter's tape
- paintbrushes
- acrylic paint in three colors
- large wall stencil stamp
- polyurethane

DIRECTIONS

1 Measure, mark, and cut floorcloth to desired size and apply a base coat of the background color. Let dry completely.

2 Fold under all edges 1 inch; press. Clip off corners on diagonal just above folds to miter; glue folded edges with tacky glue to hem.

3 Using a yardstick and pencil, measure and mark out grid pattern. Apply painter's tape to form squares of grid pattern, then apply the secondary paint color. Let dry; remove tape.

4 Pour some of the third paint color into a dish, dip stamp into paint, then press stamp onto center of every other square. Let dry.

5 Seal the floorcloth with two coats of polyurethane, letting dry between coats.

Ribbon-Trimmed Pillowcases

MATERIALS

- pillowcase
- iron
- ironing board
- 3 yards of ribbon to coordinate with pillowcase
- tape measure
- scissors
- pins
- sewing machine
- thread to match ribbon

DIRECTIONS

1 Wash, dry and iron pillowcase.

2 Measure width of pillowcase, double the width and add 1 inch. Cut a strip of ribbon to this length. Fold short ends of ribbon under ½ inch; press.

3 Position ribbon around pillowcase about 3 inches from open end; pin in place.

4 Sew ribbon to pillowcase, stitching in place along one side of ribbon. Then stitch along other side. Press.

Wooden Planter

[SKILL LEVEL: BEGINNER]

MATERIALS

- unfinished wooden window planter box
- 150-grit sandpaper
- tack cloth
- primer
- 3½-inch-wide paintbrush
- green latex paint
- 2-inch-wide paintbrushes
- two precut square wooden blocks
- yellow acrylic paint
- vintage poster stickers
- 6x8-inch chalkboard
- glue

DIRECTIONS

1 Start with a ready-made, unfinished wooden window planter box *(ours is 25 inches long by 8 inches tall by 11 inches deep)*. Sand the box first with coarse sandpaper, then with fine, until all sides of the box are smooth. Wipe off the sawdust with tack cloth. Apply primer (ours was tinted to match the paint) to the box with a 3½-inch-wide paintbrush and let dry. Apply green latex paint to the box with a 3½-inch-wide paintbrush. Let dry. Rinse out your brush with soap and hot water. Using 2-inch-wide paintbrushes, paint two precut square wooden blocks *(ours are 4½x4½ inches each)* with yellow acrylic paint. Set aside and let dry.

2 Cut one or more vintage-poster stickers into small strips. Peeling the backs off the stickers, apply the pieces randomly to create a collage of strips on the wooden border of a 6x8-inch chalkboard. Glue down any portion of a strip that does not hold firmly in place. Peel off the backing of one whole sticker and place on a dry, painted wooden block. Repeat for the other block.

3 Mount both wooden blocks and the chalkboard onto your planter with wood glue. Position the collaged chalkboard front and center on your planter, and place each wooden block about 2 inches from either side. Place pansies or other flowers inside. For a personalized touch, write the name of your flowers or whatever wording you choose on your chalkboard.

Starfish-Embellished Planter

MATERIALS
- selection of shells and starfish
- pencil
- sap bucket
- epoxy

DIRECTIONS

1 Select a sufficient number of shells or starfish to create a symmetrical design.

2 With a pencil, lightly mark a dot for the positions of the shells or starfish to form a border around the sap bucket at the desired place.

3 Mix the epoxy.

4 Hold a shell or starfish against the bucket to observe the points of contact between the shell and bucket. Apply epoxy to a shell or starfish at contact points, then press it onto the bucket and hold until the epoxy dries. Repeat with the other shells or starfish until the design is complete.

Outdoor Candleholder

DIRECTIONS

1 Draw dots in a sun design on a piece of paper.

2 Tape a piece of saral paper to the face of the bucket. Tape the pattern over the saral paper. Use a pencil to draw over the existing dots on the design and transfer the design to the bucket. Remove the paper pattern and saral paper. Use the pencil to retrace any dot that you can't clearly see on the bucket. Repeat this process on the other side of the bucket if desired.

3 If possible, ask for help from a partner to hold the bucket securely on its side with the pattern facing up. Wearing safety glasses, and with the bucket firmly held in place, drill holes through the marks of the pattern.

4 Place the candle inside the bucket.

MATERIALS
- paper
- pencil
- tape
- saral paper
- sap bucket
- safety glasses
- drill with 1/8-inch bit
- pillar candle

Cork Coasters

MATERIALS

- roll of cork liner
- circular cutter
- rubber sheeting
  (available at craft stores)
- craft knife
- scissors
- leaves
- latex or acrylic paint
- foam brush
- wax paper *(optional)*
- brayer *(optional)*
- satin polyurethane

DIRECTIONS

1 Set the circle cutter to create circles about 3½ to 4 inches in diameter and cut the desired number of coasters from the cork liner.

2 Trace around a cork liner on rubber sheeting to create an equal number of backs for coasters. Cut out the rubber backs with scissors.

3 Peel off the backing from the cork circles and affix one to each of the rubber backs.

4 Pour a small amount of latex or acrylic paint into a dish, dip the foam brush into the paint and apply to the back of a leaf. Press the leaf onto a coaster top to leave an impression and carefully remove. For a crisp image, top the leaf with wax paper and roll over the leaf with a brayer. Carefully lift off the paper and leaf.

5 Seal your handiwork with a coat of polyurethane. Let dry.

Tray Liner

DIRECTIONS

1 Measure the length and width of the inside of the tray and subtract ¼ inch from each measurement. Measure and mark a rectangle on the foam core to these measurements, then cut out the rectangle with a craft knife, using a metal yardstick as straightedge.

2 Cut several ribbon strips equal to the width of the napkin plus 1 inch. Wrap napkin around the foam core, folding the ends over the short edges. Use fabric glue to secure the short edges in place.

3 Arrange ribbons, spaced as desired, across the top of napkin so they extend ½ inch past each edge, then fold the ends under and glue in place. Occasionally check distance between ribbons to keep the lines straight and evenly spaced.

4 When all ribbons have been applied, fold the flaps under along the long edges and glue in place. To secure, place tacks through the fabric into the foam core. Ideally, flaps along the long edges will abut neatly or overlap on the underside. If not, fill the gap with a strip of the wide ribbon. Turn over and place in tray.

MATERIALS

- tray
- tape measure
- ¼-inch-thick foam core
- pencil
- metal yardstick
- craft knife
- large napkin
- scissors
- about 4½ yards of ribbon in two widths and colors
- fabric glue
- tacks

picture
perfect

E VEN IF YOUR PHOTOS, POSTERS, prints or collectibles aren't masterworks of art, there's no reason why you shouldn't display them with style. You don't have to purchase expensive custom frames to do so. Just use your imagination and fashion a frame yourself. A personalized frame not only adds decorative dimension to your decor, it can also serve as an artistic statement in itself.

The humblest of materials can yield a lovely frame—strips of ribbon, corrugated cardboard, buttons, even the shards of a broken ceramic plate. You can also customize low-cost unfinished frames with paint or stain to complement the colors in a room; hinge three frames together to form a charming triptych; or add three-dimensional patterns to an old frame with sculpting compound. Fine old frames are plentiful at flea markets. Why not pick up a few, unify them with whitewash, and use them to display a collection of family photos or children's drawings?

If you have no artwork to speak of, then go ahead and make a few. Gather a collection of leaves or flowers, press and preserve them in glycerin, then frame them en masse like a collection of botanical prints. Create a pretty tableau of seashells and colorful stones in a shadow box. Or, frame floral fabric remnants and display them as a group or separately as single dramatic panels.

Shadow Box

MATERIALS

- wooden frame with glass
- ruler
- pencil
- saw
- 1x4 lumber
- wood glue
- hammer
- panel nails
- acrylic paint in two colors
- 1-inch foam brush
- medium-grit sandpaper
- three ¾-inch hinges with screws
- screwdriver
- painter's tape
- liner brush or liner tool *(available at art-supply stores)*
- ¼-inch plywood or scrap of beadboard (for back)

DIRECTIONS

1 Measure frame. Cut and saw lumber to create top, bottom, sides and shelf of the shadow box to fit behind frame opening. Glue pieces together, then nail them in place.

2 Paint frame and box in lightest color. Let dry.

3 Paint frame and box in darkest color. Let dry.

4 Distress top coat of paint with sandpaper.

5 Attach frame to box on one side with hinges.

6 Mask off box with tape around frame edge, dip stamp in medium color of paint, then randomly apply to edges of frame. Remove tape.

7 Cut plywood (or beadboard) to fit back of box. Paint it the lightest color, then, using liner brush, paint on faux beadboard lines with the darkest color of paint. Let dry.

8 Glue back to box, then nail in place.

Beribboned Borders

MATERIALS
- white foam core
- craft knife
- ruler
- scissors
- ribbons
- glue

DIRECTIONS

1 Cut foam core into desired frame sizes with craft knife against straightedge.

2 Cut strips of ribbon approximately 1½ inches longer than sides of frame.

3 Lightly glue ribbon to front, overlapping ends of horizontal sides over vertical ones. Wrap ribbon ends over to back of foam core and glue in place. (Before applying ribbon to frame, test glue on ribbon to see if it causes ribbon to discolor or bleed—if it does, apply glue to ribbon only on back of frame.)

4 Cut out your images, apply glue to backs and center on foam core backing, which will look like matting.

Carved Clay Frame

[SKILL LEVEL: BEGINNER]

MATERIALS

- 1-pound box of Super Sculpey sculpting compound
- rolling pin
- cutting board
- craft knife
- pencil
- old frame with simple beveled border
- extra-thick tacky glue
- 1-inch foam brushes
- acrylic paint in two colors

DIRECTIONS

1 Work clay in hands to soften. Roll flat to a ³⁄₁₆-inch thickness.

2 Cut out leaf shapes with craft knife. To make stems, roll strands about ¼-inch in diameter. Flatten and curve them slightly to fit within molding of the frame.

3 Use a pencil point to scratch in leaf veins.

4 Follow package instructions to harden the clay.

5 After shapes harden, glue them onto frame. Let dry.

6 Paint frame with a wash of paint (two parts of darker color of paint to one part water). Let dry.

7 Apply a wash of the lighter color (two parts paint to two parts water) to highlight.

Toney Triptych

DIRECTIONS

1 Paint frames and let dry.

2 Varnish frames and let dry.

3 Connect each frame with two hinges. Mount the hinges with pivot facing outward.

MATERIALS

- three identical straight-sided wooden frames
- acrylic paint in three complementary colors
- paintbrush
- varnish
- four 1-inch hinges and screws
- screwdriver
- ruler

Mini-Mosaic Frame

DIRECTIONS

1 Sand or plane down outside edge of frame to form 45-degree beveled edges approximately ¼ inch wide.

2 Paint frame and let dry.

3 Wrap tiles in a towel. Then, wearing safety glasses, shatter them with a hammer.

4 Following instructions, apply adhesive to tiles and place them on frame about ¹⁄₆ inch to ¹⁄₈ inch apart. Let dry overnight.

5 Then, wearing rubber gloves, apply grout, following instructions. Remove any residue with a moist sponge.

MATERIALS
- wooden frame
- plane or coarse sandpaper with sanding block
- acrylic paint
- paintbrush
- safety glasses
- tiles
- towel
- hammer
- adhesive
- rubber gloves
- white grout
- rubber float or moist sponge

Textured Two-Tone Frame

[SKILL LEVEL: BEGINNER]

DIRECTIONS

1 Sand or plane down outside edge of the frame to form 45-degree beveled edges approximately ¼ inch-wide.

2 Apply dimensional paint to the top surface of the frame in stripes as shown in the photo.

3 Let dry (follow manufacturer's instructions for drying time). Paint the rest of the frame with acrylic paint. Let dry.

MATERIALS
- wooden frame
- plane or coarse sandpaper with sanding block
- dimensional paint
- acrylic paint
- paintbrush

Button Border Frame

MATERIALS
- wooden frame
- acrylic paint
- paintbrush
- frame
- glue
- various buttons

DIRECTIONS

1 Paint frame with acrylic paint. Let dry.

2 Arrange buttons as desired on front surface of frame.

3 Lift the buttons one by one, apply a drop of glue to the back, and secure into place. Let dry.

Corrugated Frame

MATERIALS

- foam core
- craft knife
- hot-glue gun
- natural corrugated paper
- acrylic paint
- paintbrush
- 2 yards of ⅛-inch-thick green leather string (or use natural leather string and paint it)
- ruler
- drill with 3/16-inch bit

DIRECTIONS

1 Cut foam core to desired frame shape (*ours is 9x12 inches with a 2-inch-wide border*).

2 Cut another piece of foam core for back that's ¼-inch smaller than outside edge of front, and glue this piece to front.

3 Paint corrugated paper with acrylic paint. Let dry.

4 Cut two 3½x12-inch strips of corrugated paper. Then cut two 3½x9-inch strips.

5 Center 9-inch lengths over top and bottom edges of frame and hot-glue in place. Turn frame over and cut inside edges of border along side of frame to allow you to turn the ¾-inch excess around to back. Glue inner edges in place. Then turn outside edges around to the back.

6 Center 12-inch lengths over sides of frame, but do not glue. Using the craft knife and ruler, create mitered corners by cutting through both layers of paper from inside corner to outside corner at each corner. Glue long borders in place as in Step 5.

7 At each corner, drill four holes, equally spaced, through frame along each side of corner cuts. Lace leather string through holes and glue to secure in back.

Pressed Leaves in Painted Frames

MATERIALS

- picture frames of various sizes
- selection of leaves
- hammer or spoon
- liquid glycerin
- paper towels
- one or two rolls of cork liner
- pencil
- craft knife
- metal ruler or yardstick
- glue
- cream-colored paper

DIRECTIONS

1 Collect mature leaves in various shapes and shades of green. Dust off excess dirt, cut ends of stems and, with a hammer or the back of a spoon, crush stem ends.

2 Heat liquid glycerin in a container to 130° to 140°F in the microwave. Place the leaves in the container, and let them remain there for a few days or up to three weeks. When the leaves darken and become supple, remove, place on paper towels, and let dry.

3 Remove backing and glass from frames. Trace the backing of a frame onto the cork liner, then use a craft knife and straightedge to cut the liner to create a mat. Measure and mark the opening so that the mat border is 1 to 2 inches all around and large enough to show the entire leaf. Use the craft knife and ruler to cut out the opening. Mark and cut a sheet of cream-colored paper in same manner, but do not cut an opening.

4 Sparingly apply dots of glue to the back of a leaf, then press it onto the center of cream-colored paper.

5 Place the cork mat facedown on the glass inside the frame, then insert the paper with attached leaf, followed by the backing, securing in place. Repeat these directions for additional leaves and frames as desired.

Framed Fabric Remnants

MATERIALS

- one or more large frames
- primer
- paintbrushes
- 180-grit sandpaper
- tack cloth
- semigloss paint or stain of single color *(optional)*
- polyurethane *(optional)*
- ½ to 1 yard of one or more floral fabrics
- metal yardstick
- pencil
- scissors
- large piece or pieces of heavy cardboard or ¼-inch-thick foam core
- craft knife
- spray glue
- brads
- hammer
- mounting cleat, picture wire, and screw eyes *(optional)*
- 1½- to 2-inch nails
- picture hooks

DIRECTIONS

1 If you plan to mount a collection of framed fabric remnants, consider painting or staining all of the frames the same color to create a unified effect. Similarly, choose fabrics that share the same essential color palette—yellow, white, and red, for example, or green, pink, and white.

2 If your frames are unfinished and you want to paint them, apply a base coat of primer; let dry. Sand lightly, then wipe off dust with tack cloth. Then, apply two coats of semigloss paint, letting dry between coats, and sanding lightly and wiping off dust after the first coat. If you're staining, apply stain directly to the frames, following manufacturer's instructions. If you're staining prefinished frames, you'll need to sand off the previous finish before staining. Apply a coat of polyurethane to stained frames; let dry.

3 Measure the inside dimensions of your frame or frames. Measure and mark your fabric to these dimensions, plus 1 inch all around, making sure to center the fabric's pattern repeat. Cut the square or rectangular piece of fabric.

4 Measure and mark the inner frame dimensions on the cardboard or foam core. Using the straightedge of a metal yardstick and a craft knife, cut the cardboard or foam core.

5 Apply spray glue to the back of the fabric, then carefully place the cardboard or foam core on the fabric, leaving 1-inch borders all around. Clip off the corners of the fabric on the diagonal, then fold over the excess fabric to the back of the cardboard or foam core.

6 Insert fabric panel in frame, insert backing if you have it, then tap in brads all around the inner frame, leaving about ¼ to ½ inch of brad extending from frame over panel edges to secure it in place. Add a mounting cleat or picture wire to frame, and hang framed panel on a picture hook.

storage
& display

Who can't benefit from a little extra storage? There's hardly a room in the house where odds and ends don't accumulate without a proper place to gather. Whether it's brushes, loofahs, and magazines in the bathroom; keys, business cards, and coins in an entryway; or buttons, scissors, needles, and thread in a sewing room—stuff has a way of just piling up or spreading out. With a little ingenuity, however, you can corral these unsightly bits and pieces into a semblance of order by fabricating storage elements that are practical and inexpensive—and stylish, too.

Instead of installing costly shelves or built-ins in a bathroom, for example, why not dress up a few aluminum buckets or wicker baskets with drawstring fabric liners, and use them as places to stow morning reading materials, shampoo or washcloths? Rather than let papers and notes pile up in an office, craft a creative message board from an old shutter or picture frame to put important reminders in plain sight. When you spruce up an old cabinet for kids' stuff or sew a satchel for makeup, lingerie, or jewelry, you won't just create an appealing accent, you'll give your family—and yourself—an incentive to keep everything in its place, too.

Decoupage Sewing Box

DIRECTIONS

1 Remove drawers and drawer hardware from storage piece. Sand drawer fronts and chest to smooth previous finish or paint. Wipe off dust with tack cloth and apply base coat of primer. Let dry thoroughly.

2 Apply two coats of the deeper shade of paint to the drawer fronts, letting dry completely between coats.

3 To create depth, mask off a small rectangle on each drawer front with painter's tape. Then apply a coat of the lighter shade of paint inside the rectangle; let dry.

4 Use foam brush to apply a coat of polyurethane to drawer fronts; let dry.

5 Measure, mark and cut a piece of wallpaper to fit over sides and top of unit. It should be wide enough to allow excess to be folded over front edges surrounding drawers.

6 Use foam brush to apply liquid adhesive to back of wallpaper. Place wallpaper on sides and top, aligning ends at base of unit. Hold in place several minutes and smooth any bubbles. Fold wallpaper over to front of unit, clipping corners at top to miter. Measure, mark and cut additional strips for interstitial areas between drawers; apply adhesive to backs and press into place. Let dry for an hour.

7 Cut several ½-inch lengths of the wooden dowel. Use epoxy to glue cut dowel pieces to center of drawers; let dry. Apply epoxy to each dowel front and attach buttons.

MATERIALS
- unfinished or used storage unit
- screwdriver
- 180-grit sandpaper
- tack cloth
- primer
- paintbrushes
- semigloss latex paint in two colors
- painter's tape
- polyurethane
- shell buttons
- wallpaper
- liquid adhesive or all-in-one sealer
- scissors
- foam brush
- buttons
- saw
- wooden dowel
- epoxy

Multipurpose Storage System

[SKILL LEVEL: BEGINNER]

MATERIALS

- wood shutter
- 220-grit sandpaper
- tack cloth
- paintbrush
- acrylic paint in desired color
- square of thin magnetic metal about 3 inches narrower than shutter width
- hammer
- four small nails
- pencil
- drill with ³/₁₆-inch bit
- three drawer pulls
- screwdriver
- sawtooth picture hook and picture hanger *(optional)*

DIRECTIONS

1 Sand shutter; wipe off dust with tack cloth.

2 Apply two or more coats of paint to all surfaces, letting dry after each coat.

3 Center metal sheet over lower section of shutter; nail in place.

4 Mark placement of three holes, evenly spaced, along lower edge of shutter. Drill a hole through shutter at each mark.

5 Screw a drawer pull into each hole. Lean shutter against a wall, or tack sawtooth picture hook to shutter, and mount on a nail or picture hanger.

Decorative Organizer

DIRECTIONS

1 Remove backing and glass from frame. Measure inside of frame or use backing to trace inside measurements on foam core and cork liner. Use craft knife and straightedge to cut foam core and cork liner to these dimensions.

2 Peel backing off liner and carefully affix to foam core. Measure width and length of foam core and divide each by 8. Using these measurements, mark along the top, bottom and sides to divide each edge in 1/8 segments.

3 Measure diagonally across the foam core from the second mark along one short side to the first mark along the opposite side, add 3 inches, and cut four ribbons to this length. Then measure diagonally across from the third mark along one short side to the fourth mark along the opposite long side, add 3 inches and cut four ribbons to this length. Firmly stretch the ribbons across the base in the same manner, folding over excess and taping to the back. Apply all ribbons going in one direction first, then the other. Press thumbtacks into ribbons at intersections.

4 Place corkboard into frame, insert backing, and secure in place.

MATERIALS
- frame no more than 20 inches wide
- metal yardstick or ruler
- pencil
- 1/4-inch-thick foam core
- craft knife
- roll of cork drawer liner
- ribbon
- scissors
- tape
- thumbtacks

Revolving Art Gallery

MATERIALS

- oversize frame
- canvas
- scissors
- staple gun
- paintbrushes
- primer
- latex paint in three colors
- painter's tape

DIRECTIONS

1 Cut a piece of canvas to fit the center of the frame plus 2 inches on all sides. Stretch the piece of canvas across the back of the frame, and attach it to the frame using a staple gun. Start stapling at the center of one side, then on the center of the opposite side. Proceed in the same manner on the two remaining perpendicular sides. Continue in this manner, stapling about 2 to 3 inches apart and finishing at the corners.

2 Apply primer to frame and canvas; let dry. Paint entire frame and canvas with dominant color paint. Let dry fully.

3 Tape off segments, equal to about ⅓ the length of the side of the frame, at the center of each side. Paint these areas with the darkest color; let dry. Remove tape.

4 Tape off segments, equal to about ⅙ the length of the side of the frame, on either side of the central painted areas. Paint these areas with the medium shade of paint; let dry. Remove tape.

5 Use pushpins and tacks to hold favorite memos, mementos, and paper artwork.

Fabric-Lined Storage Container

[SKILL LEVEL: BEGINNER]

MATERIALS

- pencil
- kraft paper or newspaper
- scissors
- about ½ yard of desired fabric
- 9-inch-tall bucket
- pins
- thread
- sewing machine
- 1 yard of cording
- safety pin
- tape
- glue

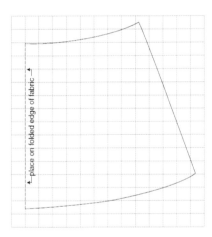

ONE SQUARE = 1 INCH

HOW TO ENLARGE PATTERNS

Using a ruler and colored pencil, mark a grid on the pattern by connecting grid lines around the edges. On a sheet of paper, mark a grid of 1-inch squares (or size given), making the same number of squares as on the pattern. An easy way to do this is to use graph paper with 1-inch squares. In each square, draw the same lines as in the corresponding square on the pattern. Another way to enlarge patterns is by using a photocopier.

DIRECTIONS

1 Enlarge template for liner, below (see How to Enlarge Patterns below), which can be scaled to fit a 9-inch-tall bucket.

2 Trace templates onto kraft paper or newspaper and cut out. NOTE: *If you use a bucket of a different size, make your own pattern by placing the bucket on its side on top of a sheet of kraft paper or newspaper, aligning the seam of bucket in one corner of paper.* Trace along the side of the bucket near the seam, then roll the bucket across the paper, tracing along the upper edge of the bucket's natural arc as you roll and stopping when the seam meets the paper on the other side. Trace another line parallel along the opposite side. Then roll the bucket back, tracing along the lower edge of the bucket's arc until you reach the other side. Draw another line ½ inch from the side edges and bottom of pattern all around for a seam allowance and 2½ inches along top for flap and seam allowance. Cut out pattern. Wrap pattern around bucket to be sure it fits accurately. If not, add to or subtract from one edge of the pattern as needed. Trace bottom circumference of bucket onto kraft paper or newspaper, draw another circle ½ inch outward from first all around for seam allowance, and cut out.

3 Pin both patterns onto fabric and cut out fabric.

4 Fold each side ½ inch in toward wrong side of fabric and press. Press a ½-inch double hem along upper edge of arced fabric, pin, and topstitch in place; remove pins. Fold fabric in half, right sides facing, sides aligned, and pin in place. Stitch sides together, starting at the bottom and stopping about 1½ inches from top edge. Remove pins.

5 With right sides facing, pin bottom to the body fabric and stitch around the circumference. Remove pins.

6 Clip into seam allowance around base 1-inch increments to ensure that the fabric lies neatly inside.

7 Fasten a safety pin to the end of the cord, and bind it with a piece of tape. Insert tape-wrapped pin through opening at one side of hemmed top edge. Pull the cord through the hem, gathering the fabric and inching the cord around the hem, until you can pull it out through the other side.

8 Place liner inside the bucket, wrong side of fabric toward inside of bucket, and turn top edge of liner over top edge of bucket.

9 Draw the cord so it's even on both sides and tie it in a bow. Trim excess cord as desired. To prevent unraveling, dip ends of cord in glue.

Colorful Cabinet

MATERIALS

- unfinished or used glass-fronted cabinet
- screwdriver
- 180-grit sandpaper
- tack cloth
- semigloss latex paint in two colors
- paintbrushes
- yardstick or ruler
- pencil
- wallpaper
- polyurethane
- scissors
- liquid adhesive or all-in-one sealer
- foam brush
- posterboard
- craft knife
- brads
- hammer

DIRECTIONS

1 Remove hardware from cabinet.

2 Sand cabinet to smooth or remove any previous paint or finish. Wipe off dust with tack cloth. Then apply a coat of primer. Let dry.

3 Paint the door front with one color of paint; let dry. Paint any trim with white or complementary color of paint; let dry. Finish with a coat of polyurethane. Let dry.

4 Measure, mark and cut a piece of wallpaper to cover both sides and top of cabinet.

5 Use foam brush to apply adhesive to back of wallpaper, apply wallpaper to cabinet, holding in place for several minutes and smoothing out any bubbles. Let dry for an hour.

6 To add interest to the front of the cabinet, measure, mark and cut a piece of wallpaper to fit the inside of the glass door. Cut a piece of posterboard to the same size. Using small nails or brads, fasten the wallpaper posterboard onto the inside of the door like a picture in a frame. Replace hardware.

Travel Makeup Bag

[SKILL LEVEL: BEGINNER]

DIRECTIONS

1 Fold one short end of place mat over, right sides facing out, leaving ¼ of place mat at one end uncovered by folded-over side. Pin in place.

2 Stitch in the ditch along the bound edges of border of the place mat along both pinned sides. Remove pins.

3 To determine placement of button, fold over the free flap, then hand-sew button in place.

4 Fold the cord or ribbon in half to form button closure, and hand-sew in place to lining at center of flap, making sure not to sew through front of flap. Clip excess cording.

MATERIALS

- quilted place mat
- pins
- matching thread
- sewing machine
- needle
- button
- 4 inches of cording or ¼-inch-wide ribbon

Sources

America Retold
(518) 589-6522
www.americaretold.com

Brother International
(800) 4-A-BROTHER
www.brother.com

Cath Kidston
(212) 343-0223
www.cathkidston.com

Cyber Island Shops
(888) 974-3557
www.cyberislandshops.com

Duck Products
(800) 321-0253
www.duckproducts.com

Fairfield Processing Corp.
(203) 744-2090
www.poly-fil.com

Garnet Hill
(800) 870-3513
www.garnethill.com

Husqvarna Viking
(800) 358-0001
www.husqvarnaviking.com

Ikea
(800) 434-4532
www.ikea-usa.com

Mastercraft Woodworking Co.
(610) 926-1500
www.mastercraftwoodworking.com

Milli Home
(212) 643-8850
www.millihome.com

Oilcloth International
(323) 344-3967
www.oilcloth.com

Pratt & Lambert
(800) BUY-PRATT
www.prattandlambert.com

Robert Allen
(416) 934-1330
www.robertallendesign.com

Susan Sargent
(800) 245-4767
www.susansargent.com

Plaid
(800) 842-4197
www.plaidonline.com

Shelterstyle.com
(713) 461-2063
www.shelterstyle.com

The Stencil Library
(800) 357-4954
www.stencil-library.com

Stroheim & Romann
(718) 706-7000
www.stroheim.com

Waverly
(800) 423-5881
www.waverly.com

Glossary

BIAS: Diagonal to the grain of a piece of fabric

BRAD: A thin, short finishing nail with a small diameter head and shank of no longer than 1½ inches

DECORATOR FABRIC: Upholstery- or drapery-weight printed or woven fabric

EMBROIDERY NEEDLE: A long needle with an eye large enough for heavy darning or embroidery thread

FOAM CORE: Two layers of paperboard between which is a layer of rigid foam

MOUNTING CLEAT: A short metal strip with a sawtooth edge that can be nailed to a picture frame for mounting

LATTICE: A lath, or narrow, thin strip of wood, usually about ¼ inch thick and ranging from ⅝ inch to 3 inches wide

PATTERN REPEAT: The interval between the repetition of the same pattern

PICTURE WIRE: Braided wire for supporting framed pictures. Choose one rated to have at least four times the breaking strength of the weight of your framed picture

RUNNING STITCH: One of a series of small, even hand stitches that run in and out between two points; sometimes called a "walking stitch," it is used for fine detail, outlining, and quickly covering space between separate design elements

SCREW EYE: A woodscrew having its shank bent into a ring

SLIP STITCH: A loose stitch catching only a thread or two of fabric; designed to be invisible from the right side

STITCH IN THE DITCH: A sewing technique, often used in machine and hand-quilting, in which stitches are made in the "ditch" formed by the turn of the cloth made when the seams of pieced fabrics are pressed to one side, thus enabling the completed stitched line to be almost invisible

TAILOR'S CHALK: Chalk used by tailors to make temporary marks on cloth

TUFTING: The fabric of an upholstered piece that is stitched repeatedly at regularly spaced indentations to secure the padding

VALANCE: An ornamental drapery treatment, usually made of fabric, typically no longer than 20 inches in numerous styles

WALKING FOOT: A big foot that has feed dogs that help feed the top layer of your fabric through, the same way the feed dogs on your machine feed the bottom layer through. If you want to do quilting in straight lines, it can be very useful, helping you avoid accidental "pleats" of fabric on the top or bottom. If you don't have one, first try sewing with your regular presser foot—just use a longer stitch than normal, and practice on a scrap to see if you need to adjust the tension in your top or bottom thread

ZIPPER FOOT: A specialty sewing machine foot that enables you to sew a line of stitches close to the edge of a zipper or encased piping

Credits

PROJECT DESIGNS: pp. 2, 6, 8, 14–15, 20–21, 22–23, 24–25, 26–27, 28–29, 68–69, 100, Ingrid Leess; pp. 10–11, 18–19, 72–74, 98–99, 102–103, 106–107, Matthew Mead Productions; pp. 12–13, 30, 34–35, 36–37, 38–39, 40–41, 42–43, 44–45, 46–47, 50, 52–53, 54–55, 56–57, 58–59, 94–95; Jean Nayar; 16–17, 32–33, 48–49, 60–61, 62–63, 70, 75, 78–79, 80–81, 92–93, 96, 101, 104–105, 108–109, Jean Nayar and Emily Reaman; pp. 64, 71, 82, 84–85, 86–87, 88–89, 90–91, Brent Pallas; pp. 66–67, 76–77, Ilana Schweber and Lindsey Emery

PHOTOGRAPHS: front cover, back cover top row, middle row, bottom row right, pp. 2, 8, 14, 17, 21, 22, 24, 25, 27, 28, 32, 49, 50, 53, 55, 56, 58, 61, 62, 66–67, 68, 70, 75, 76–77, 78–79, 80–81, 92, 96, 100–101, 105, 108, Aimee Herring; pp. 6, 11, 18, 72–74, 98, 102, 106, Eric Roth; back cover bottom row left, pp. 12–13, 30, 35, 36, 39, 41, 43, 45–46, 82, 84–85, 86–87, 88–89, 90, 95, Marcus Tullis; pp. 64, 71, John Gould Bessler

Product Information

PP. 10–11: paint, Grasshopper 1544 from Pratt & Lambert and Reed 1656 from Behr; wallpaper, from Susan Sargent's Home Collection; adhesive/sealer, Mod Podge from Plaid.

PP. 12–13: cabinet, Glass Door Display Cabinet, #9009 from Mastercraft; paint, Folk Art in Lemon Custard, Taffy, Burgundy and Holiday Red from Plaid; wallpaper, Penrose Companion, #572822, from the Waverly Lifestyles collection from Waverly.

PP. 16–17: cork, Easy Liner from Duck Products.

PP. 18–19: paint, Lilac Phlox #1133, Geneva Blue #1135, Half Tone #2298, Pratt & Lambert; liquid adhesive/sealer, Mod Podge, Plaid.

PP. 34–35: fabric, Ile de France, in Grasse, from Robert Allen.

PP. 36–37: fabric, Flamonde, in Azure, border fabric, Somme, in Azure, from Robert Allen.

PP. 38–39: fabric, Wakaya, in Ivory, Robert Allen.

PP. 44–45: fabric, Arbor Rose, in Petal, from Waverly.

PP. 46–47: fabric, Vignette, in Periwinkle, Linen Dot, Violet, from Robert Allen.

PP. 48–49: organza place mats, from Milli Home.

PP. 54–55: fabrics, Retablos Washed Denim, Santa Ponza crewel-embroidered fabric, Santeros Washed Denim; fringe, #0107L0530, all from Stroheim & Romann.

PP. 56–57: Indian Washed denim Stripe, Retablos Washed Denim, Santeros Washed Denim, Ortega Washed Denim, Santa Fe Washed Denim, Palm Embroidered Denim, Cores Washed Denim, Rancho Quilted Denim, all from Stroheim & Romann.

PP. 58–59: fabrics, Ortega, Indian Denim Stripe, from Stroheim & Romann.

PP. 60–61: place mats, from Milli Home.

PP. 62–63: place mats, from Milli Home

P. 74: paint, Old Linen, Melon Green, from Pratt & Lambert; Crushed Ice, from Behr.

PP. 78–79: buckets, from Shelterstyle.com

P. 80: cork, Easy Liner from Duck Products.

P. 84: paint, Folk Art in wicker White, Bayberry and Tapioca, from Plaid.

P. 86: paint, Folk Art in Cinnamon and Tapioca, Plaid.

P. 89: dimensional paint, Fashion Dimensional in white, from Plaid.

PP. 92–93: cork, Easy Liner, from Duck Products.

PP. 98–99: paint, Coral Pink 1894 and Half Tone 2298 from Pratt & Lambert; wallpaper, Good Catch, from Carey Lind; adhesive/sealer, Mod Podge, from Plaid.

P. 101: cork, Easy Liner, from Duck Products.

PP. 102–103: paint, 247-4 Velvet Morning, 348-3 Blue Thistle, 346-3 Debonaire, from Pittsburgh Paint.

PP. 104–105: bucket, from Shelterstyle.com.

PP. 106–107: paint, Old Linen and White, from Pratt & Lambert; wallpaper, Please Don't Eat the Daisy, from Carey Lind.

PP. 108–109: place mat, Milli Home.